ㅏ尺丹几乙ㄴ丹ㅏと

Translated Language Learning

The Little Mermaid

小美人鱼

Hans Christian Andersen

English / 普通话

Copyright © 2023 Tranzlaty
All rights reserved.
Published by Tranzlaty
ISBN: 978-1-83566-289-2
Original text by Hans Christian Andersen
Den Lille Havfrue
First published in Danish in 1837
www.tranzlaty.com

The Little Mermaid
小美人鱼

Far out in the ocean, where the water is blue
在遥远的海洋中,那里的水是蓝色的

here the water is as blue as the prettiest cornflower
这里的水像最漂亮的矢车菊一样蓝

and the water is as clear as the purest crystal
水像最纯净的水晶一样清澈

this water, far out in the ocean is very, very deep
这片水,在遥远的海洋中非常非常深

water so deep, indeed, that no cable could reach the bottom
事实上,水是如此之深,以至于没有电缆可以到达底部

you could pile many church steeples upon each other
你可以把许多教堂的尖顶堆在一起

but they would not reach the surface of the water
但它们不会到达水面

There dwell the Sea King and his subjects
那里住着海王和他的臣民

you might think it is just bare yellow sand at the bottom
你可能会认为它只是底部光秃秃的黄沙

but we must not imagine that there is nothing there
但我们不能想象那里什么都没有

on this sand grow the strangest flowers and plants
在这片沙地上生长着最奇怪的花草

and you can't imagine how pliant the leaves and stems are
你无法想象叶子和茎有多柔韧

the slightest agitation of the water causes them to stir
水最轻微的搅动会引起它们搅动

it is as if each leaf had a life of their own
仿佛每片叶子都有自己的生命

Fishes, both large and small, glide between the branches
大大小小的鱼在树枝之间滑行
just like when birds fly among the trees here upon land
就像鸟儿在陆地上的树林中飞翔一样

In the deepest spot of all stands a beautiful castle
在最深处矗立着一座美丽的城堡
this beautiful castle is the castle of the Sea King
这座美丽的城堡是海王的城堡
the walls of the castle are built of coral
城堡的墙壁是用珊瑚建造的
and the long Gothic windows are of the clearest amber
长长的哥特式窗户是最清晰的琥珀色
The roof of the castle is formed of sea shells
城堡的屋顶由贝壳组成
and the shells open and close as the water flows over them
当水流过它们时，贝壳会打开和关闭
Their appearance is more beautiful than can be described
它们的外表比描述的更美丽
within each shell there lies a glittering pearl
每个贝壳里都有一颗闪闪发光的珍珠
and each pearl would be fit for the diadem of a queen
每颗珍珠都适合女王的王冠

The Sea King had been a widower for many years
海王多年来一直是鳏夫
and his aged mother kept house for him
他年迈的母亲为他打理房子
She was a very sensible woman
她是一个非常懂事的女人

but she was exceedingly proud of her high birth
但她为自己的高贵出身感到非常自豪
and on that account she wore twelve oysters on her tail
因此，她的尾巴上戴着十二只牡蛎
others of high rank were only allowed to wear six oysters
其他高级牡蛎只允许佩戴六只牡蛎
She was, however, deserving of very great praise
然而，她值得极大的赞美
there was something she especially deserved praise for
她特别值得称赞
she took great care of the the little sea princesses
她非常照顾小海公主
she had six granddaughters that she loved
她有六个她喜欢的孙女
all the sea princesses were beautiful children
所有的海公主都是漂亮的孩子
but the youngest sea princess was the prettiest of them
但最年轻的海公主是其中最漂亮的
Her skin was as clear and delicate as a rose leaf
她的皮肤像玫瑰叶一样清澈细腻
and her eyes were as blue as the deepest sea
她的眼睛像最深的大海一样蓝
but, like all the others, she had no feet
但是，像其他人一样，她没有脚
and at the end of her body was a fish's tail
在她身体的尽头是一条鱼尾巴

All day long they played in the great halls of the castle
他们整天在城堡的大厅里玩耍
out of the walls of the castle grew beautiful flowers
城堡的城墙上长出了美丽的花朵
and she loved to play among the living flowers, too
她也喜欢在活生生的花朵中玩耍

The large amber windows were open, and the fish swam in
琥珀色的大窗户打开了，鱼游了进来
it is just like when we leave the windows open
这就像我们打开窗户一样
and then the pretty swallows fly into our houses
然后漂亮的燕子飞进我们的房子
only the fishes swam up to the princesses
只有鱼游到公主身边
they were the only ones that ate out of their hands
他们是唯一从他们手中吃掉的人
and they allowed themselves to be stroked by them
他们允许自己被他们抚摸

Outside the castle there was a beautiful garden
城堡外面有一个美丽的花园
in the garden grew bright-red and dark-blue flowers
花园里长着鲜红色和深蓝色的花朵
and there grew blossoms like flames of fire
那里开出的花朵像火焰一样
the fruit on the plants glittered like gold
植物上的果实像金子一样闪闪发光
and the leaves and stems continually waved to and fro
叶子和茎不停地来回摆动
The earth on the ground was the finest sand
地上的大地是最好的沙子
but it does not have the colour of the sand we know
但它没有我们所知道的沙子的颜色
it is as blue as the flame of burning sulphur
它像燃烧硫磺的火焰一样蓝
Over everything lay a peculiar blue radiance
一切都散发着奇特的蓝色光芒
it is as if the blue sky were everywhere
仿佛到处都是蓝天

the blue of the sky was above and below
天空的蓝色在上面和下面
In calm weather the sun could be seen
在平静的天气里，可以看到太阳
from here the sun looked like a reddish-purple flower
从这里看，太阳看起来像一朵红紫色的花
and the light streamed from the calyx of the flower
光从花的花萼中流出

the palace garden was divided into several parts
故宫花园分为几个部分
Each of the princesses had their own little plot of ground
每个公主都有自己的小块土地
on this plot they could plant whatever flowers they pleased
在这块土地上，他们可以种植任何他们喜欢的花
one princess arranged her flower bed in the form of a whale
一位公主将她的花坛布置成鲸鱼的形状
one princess arranged her flowers like a little mermaid
一位公主像小美人鱼一样布置她的花朵
and the youngest child made her garden round, like the sun
最小的孩子把她的花园弄得圆圆的，像太阳一样
and in her garden grew beautiful red flowers
在她的花园里开着美丽的红色花朵
these flowers were as red as the rays of the sunset
这些花朵像夕阳的光芒一样红

She was a strange child; quiet and thoughtful
她是个奇怪的孩子；安静周到，
her sisters showed delight at the wonderful things
她的姊妹们对这些奇妙的事情感到高兴

the things they obtained from the wrecks of vessels
他们从船只残骸中获得的东西
but she cared only for her pretty red flowers
但她只关心她漂亮的红色花朵
although there was also a beautiful marble statue
虽然还有一尊美丽的大理石雕像
It was the representation of a handsome boy
这是一个英俊男孩的代表
it had been carved out of pure white stone
它是用纯白色的石头雕刻而成的
and it had fallen to the bottom of the sea from a wreck
它从沉船中掉到了海底
this marble statue of a boy she cared about too
这个她也很关心的男孩的大理石雕像

She planted, by the statue, a rose-colored weeping willow
她在雕像旁种了一棵玫瑰色的垂柳
and soon the willow hung its fresh branches over the statue
很快,柳树就把新鲜的树枝挂在了雕像上
the branches almost reached down to the blue sands
树枝几乎伸到蓝色的沙滩上
The shadows of the tree had the color of violet
树的阴影是紫罗兰色的
and the shadows waved to and fro like the branches
影子像树枝一样来回摆动
all of this created the most interesting illusion
所有这些都创造了最有趣的错觉
as if the crown of the tree and the roots were playing
仿佛树冠和树根在玩耍
it looked as if they were trying to kiss each other
看起来他们好像在亲吻对方

her greatest pleasure was hearing about the world above
她最大的乐趣是听到上面的世界
the world above the deep sea she lived in
她所居住的深海之上的世界
She made her old grandmother tell her all about it
她让她的老祖母告诉她这一切
the ships and the towns, the people and the animals
船只和城镇，人和动物
up there the flowers of the land had fragrance
在那儿，大地的花朵散发着芬芳
the flowers below the sea had no fragrance
海底的花朵没有香味
up there the trees of the forest were green
那里的森林树木是绿色的
and the fishes in the trees could sing beautifully
树上的鱼儿可以唱歌
up there it was a pleasure to listen to the fish
在那里，听鱼叫是一种乐趣
her grandmother called the birds fishes
她的祖母称这些鸟为鱼
else the little mermaid would not have understood
否则小美人鱼不会明白的
because the little mermaid had never seen birds
因为小美人鱼从未见过鸟

her grandmother told her about the rites of mermaids
她的祖母告诉她美人鱼的仪式
"one day you will reach your fifteenth year"
"总有一天你会年满十五岁"
"then you will have permission to go to the surface"
"那么你就有权去水面了"
"you will be able to sit on the rocks in the moonlight"
"在月光下，你将能够坐在岩石上"

"and you will see the great ships go sailing by"
"你会看到大船驶过"

"Then you will see forests and towns and the people"
"然后你会看到森林、城镇和人民"

the following year one of the sisters would be fifteen
第二年,其中一个姊妹就十五岁了

but each sister was a year younger than the other
但每个姐妹都比另一个小一岁

the youngest would have to wait five years before her turn
最小的孩子必须等五年才能轮到她

only then could she rise up from the bottom of the ocean
只有这样,她才能从海底升起

and only then could she see the earth as we do
只有这样,她才能像我们一样看到地球

However, each of the sisters made each other a promise
然而,姐妹俩都向对方许下了诺言

they were going to tell the others what they had seen
他们要告诉其他人他们所看到的

Their grandmother could not tell them enough
他们的祖母无法告诉他们足够多

there were so many things they wanted to know about
他们想知道的事情太多了

the youngest sister longed for her turn the most
最小的妹妹最渴望轮到她

but, she had to wait longer than all the others
但是,她不得不等待比其他人更长的时间

and she was so quiet and thoughtful about the world
她对这个世界是如此安静和深思熟虑

there were many nights where she stood by the open window

有很多个夜晚,她站在敞开的窗户旁
and she looked up through the dark blue water
她透过深蓝色的海水抬起头来
and she watched the fish as they splashed with their fins
她看着鱼用鳍嬉戏
She could see the moon and stars shining faintly
她能看到月亮和星星微弱地闪耀
but from deep below the water these things look different
但从水下的深处看,这些东西看起来不同
the moon and stars looked larger than they do to our eyes
月亮和星星看起来比我们眼中的要大
sometimes, something like a black cloud went past
有时,像乌云一样的东西会过去
she knew that it could be a whale swimming over her head
她知道那可能是一条鲸鱼从她头上游过
or it could be a ship, full of human beings
或者它可能是一艘船,满载着人类
human beings who couldn't imagine what was under them
无法想象他们下面是什么的人类
a pretty little mermaid holding out her white hands
一条漂亮的小美人鱼伸出她白皙的双手
a pretty little mermaid reaching towards their ship
一条漂亮的小美人鱼伸向他们的船

the day came when the eldest had her fifteenth birthday
大姐十五岁生日的那一天到了
now she was allowed to rise to the surface of the ocean
现在她被允许上升到海面

and that night she swum up to the surface
那天晚上,她游到了水面
you can imagine all the things she saw up there
你可以想象她在那里看到的所有东西
and you can imagine all the things she had to talk about
你可以想象她不得不谈论的所有事情
But the finest thing, she said, was to lie on a sand bank
但她说,最好的事情是躺在沙洲上
in the quiet moonlit sea, near the shore
在宁静的月光下,靠近海岸
from there she had gazed at the lights on the land
从那里,她凝视着大地上的灯光
they were the lights of the near-by town
他们是附近城镇的灯光
the lights had twinkled like hundreds of stars
灯光像数百颗星星一样闪烁
she had listened to the sounds of music from the town
她听着镇上传来的音乐声
she had heard noise of carriages drawn by their horses
她听见马车被他们的马拉着的声音
and she had heard the voices of human beings
她听到了人类的声音
and the had heard merry pealing of the bells
听见钟声欢快地响起
the bells ringing in the church steeples
教堂尖顶上的钟声响起
but she could not go near all these wonderful things
但她无法靠近所有这些美妙的事物
so she longed for these wonderful things all the more
所以她更加渴望这些美好的事物

you can imagine how eagerly the youngest sister listened
你可以想象最小的妹妹听得多么热切

the descriptions of the upper world were like a dream
对上层世界的描述就像一场梦

afterwards she stood at the open window of her room
之后,她站在房间敞开的窗户前

and she looked to the surface, through the dark-blue water
她透过深蓝色的海水向水面望去

she thought of the great city her sister had told her of
她想起了她姐姐告诉她的那个伟大的城市

the great city with all its bustle and noise
喧嚣和喧嚣的伟大城市

she even fancied she could hear the sound of the bells
她甚至幻想自己能听到钟声

she imagined their sound carried to the depths of the sea
她想象着他们的声音被带到大海深处

after another year the second sister had her birthday
又过了一年,二姐过生日了

she too received permission to rise to the surface
她也获得了浮出水面的许可

and from there she could swim about where she pleased
从那里,她可以游到她喜欢的地方

She had gone to the surface just as the sun was setting
她在太阳落山时浮出水面

this, she said, was the most beautiful sight of all
她说,这是最美丽的景象

The whole sky looked like a disk of pure gold
整个天空看起来就像一个纯金的圆盘

and there were violet and rose-colored clouds

还有紫罗兰色和玫瑰色的云

they were too beautiful to describe, she said
她说,它们太美了,无法形容

and she said how the clouds drifted across the sky
她说云朵是如何在天空中飘荡的

and something had flown by more swiftly than the clouds
有些东西飞得比云还快

a large flock of wild swans flew toward the setting sun
一大群野天鹅向夕阳飞去

the swans had been like a long white veil across the sea
天鹅就像一层长长的白色面纱,横跨大海

She had also tried to swim towards the sun
她还试图向太阳游去

but some distance away the sun sank into the waves
但不远处,太阳沉入海浪中

she saw how the rosy tints faded from the clouds
她看到玫瑰色的色调是如何从云层中褪去的

and she saw how the colour had also faded from the sea
她看到颜色也从海里褪色了

the next year it was the third sister's turn
第二年,轮到三姐了

this sister was the boldest of all the sisters
这位姊妹是所有姊妹中最大胆的

she swam up a broad river that emptied into the sea
她游上了一条宽阔的河流,这条河流流入大海

On the banks of the river she saw green hills
在河岸上,她看到了绿色的山丘

the green hills were covered with beautiful vines
绿色的山丘上长满了美丽的藤蔓

and on the hills there were forests of trees

山上有树林

and out of the forests palaces and castles poked out
从森林中探出宫殿和城堡

She had heard birds singing in the trees
她听见鸟儿在树上唱歌

and she had felt the rays of the sun on her skin
她感觉到阳光照在她的皮肤上

the rays were so strong that she had to dive back
光线太强了,她不得不向后潜去

and she cooled her burning face in the cool water
她用凉水冷却了她灼热的脸

In a narrow creek she found a group of little children
在一条狭窄的小溪里,她发现了一群小孩

they were the first human children she had ever seen
他们是她见过的第一个人类孩子

She wanted to play with the children too
她也想和孩子们一起玩

but the children fled from her in a great fright
但孩子们吓得从她身边逃走了

and then a little black animal came to the water
然后一只黑色的小动物来到水边

it was a dog, but she did not know it was a dog
那是一条狗,但她不知道这是一条狗

because she had never seen a dog before
因为她以前从未见过狗

and the dog barked at the mermaid furiously
狗对美人鱼愤怒地吠叫

she became frightened and rushed back to the open sea
她吓坏了,冲回了公海

But she said she should never forget the beautiful forest
但她说,她永远不应该忘记那片美丽的森林

the green hills and the pretty children
青山和漂亮的孩子

she found it exceptionally funny how they swam
她觉得他们游泳的方式非常有趣
because the little human children didn't have tails
因为人类小孩子没有尾巴
so with their little legs they kicked the water
于是他们用小腿踢了踢水

The fourth sister was more timid than the last
四姐比上一个更胆小
She had decided to stay in the midst of the sea
她决定留在海中
but she said it was as beautiful there as nearer the land
但她说，那里和离土地更近一样美丽
from the surface she could see many miles around her
从表面上看，她可以看到周围数英里
the sky above her looked like a bell of glass
她头顶的天空看起来像一个玻璃钟
and she had seen the ships sail by
她看到船只驶过
but they were at a very great distance from her
但他们离她很远
and, with their sails, they looked like sea gulls
而且，它们的帆看起来像海鸥
she saw how the dolphins played in the waves
她看到了海豚如何在海浪中嬉戏
and great whales spouted water from their nostrils
大鲸鱼从鼻孔里喷出水
like a hundred fountains all playing together
就像一百个喷泉一起玩耍

The fifth sister's birthday occurred in the winter
五姐的生日发生在冬天
so she saw things that the others had not seen
所以她看到了其他人没有看到的东西

at this time of the year the sea looked green
每年的这个时候,大海看起来都是绿色的

large icebergs were floating on the green water
巨大的冰山漂浮在绿色的水面上

and each iceberg looked like a pearl, she said
她说,每座冰山看起来都像一颗珍珠

but they were larger and loftier than the churches
但它们比教堂更大、更高

and they were of the most interesting shapes
它们的形状最有趣

and each iceberg glittered like diamonds
每座冰山都像钻石一样闪闪发光

She had seated herself on one of the icebergs
她坐在其中一座冰山上

and she let the wind play with her long hair
她让风吹拂着她的长发

She noticed something interesting about the ships
她注意到这些船有一些有趣的东西

all the ships sailed past the icebergs very rapidly
所有的船只都非常迅速地驶过冰山

and they steered away as far as they could
他们尽可能地避开

it was as if they were afraid of the iceberg
就好像他们害怕冰山一样

she stayed out at sea into the evening
她在海上呆到晚上才

the sun went down and dark clouds covered the sky
太阳下山了,乌云笼罩着天空

the thunder rolled across the ocean of icebergs
雷声滚过冰山的海洋

and the flashes of lightning glowed red on the icebergs
闪电在冰山上发出红色的光芒

and they were tossed about by the heaving sea
他们被波涛汹涌的海浪抛来抛去

all the ships the sails were trembling with fear
所有的船帆都因恐惧而颤抖
and the mermaid sat calmly on the floating iceberg
美人鱼平静地坐在漂浮的冰山上
she watched the lightning strike into the sea
她眼睁睁地看着闪电击中海里

All of her five older sisters had grown up now
她的五个姐姐现在都长大了
therefore they could go to the surface when they pleased
因此，他们可以在他们高兴的时候浮出水面
at first they were delighted with the surface world
起初，他们对地表世界感到高兴
they couldn't get enough of the new and beautiful sights
他们无法得到足够的新的和美丽的景点
but eventually they all grew indifferent towards it
但最终他们都对此漠不关心
and after a month they didn't visit much at all anymore
一个月后，他们不再来太多地方了
they told their sister it was much more beautiful at home
他们告诉姐姐，家里要漂亮得多

Yet often, in the evening hours, they did go up
然而，在傍晚时分，他们确实上升了
the five sisters twined their arms about each other
五姊妹双臂缠绕在一起
and together, arm in arm, they rose to the surface
他们手挽手一起浮出水面
often they went up when there was a storm approaching
当暴风雨来临时，他们经常上去

they feared that the storm might win a ship
他们担心风暴可能会赢得一艘船

so they swam to the vessel and sung to the sailors
于是他们游到船上,向水手们唱歌

Their voices were more charming than that of any human
他们的声音比任何人都更迷人

and they begged the voyagers not to fear if they sank
他们恳求航海者不要害怕他们沉没

because the depths of the sea was full of delights
因为大海的深处充满了欢乐

But the sailors could not understand their songs
但是水手们听不懂他们的歌

and they thought their singing was the sighing of the storm
他们认为他们的歌声是暴风雨的叹息

therefore their songs were never beautiful to the sailors
因此,他们的歌对水手来说从来都不是美妙的

because if the ship sank the men would drown
因为如果船沉没,这些人就会淹死

the dead gained nothing from the palace of the Sea King
死者从海王的宫殿中一无所获

but their youngest sister was left at the bottom of the sea
但他们最小的妹妹却被留在了海底

looking up at them, she was ready to cry
抬头看着他们,她准备哭了

you should know mermaids have no tears that they can cry
你应该知道美人鱼没有眼泪,她们可以哭泣

so her pain and suffering was more acute than ours
所以她的痛苦和苦难比我们更严重

"Oh, I wish I was also fifteen years old!" said she
"噢，我真希望我也是十五岁！"她说

"I know that I shall love the world up there"
"我知道我会爱那里的世界"

"and I shall love all the people who live in that world"
"我要爱所有生活在那个世界上的人"

but, at last, she too reached her fifteenth year
但是，最后，她也到了十五岁

"Well, now you are grown up," said her grandmother
"嗯，现在你长大了，"她的祖母说

"Come, and let me adorn you like your sisters"
"来吧，让我像你的姐妹一样装饰你"

And she placed a wreath of white lilies in her hair
她把一圈白色的百合花戴在头发上

every petal of the lilies was half a pearl
百合花的每一片花瓣都是半颗珍珠

Then, the old lady ordered eight great oysters to come
然后，老太太点了八只大牡蛎来

the oysters attached themselves to the tail of the princess
牡蛎附着在公主的尾巴上

under the sea oysters are used to show your rank
海底牡蛎是用来显示你的等级的

"But they hurt me so," said the little mermaid
"可是他们把我伤害得太厉害了，"小美人鱼说

"Yes, I know oysters hurt," replied the old lady
"是的，我知道牡蛎很痛，"老太太回答说

"but you know very well that pride must suffer pain"
"但你很清楚，骄傲必须承受痛苦"

how gladly she would have shaken off all this grandeur
她会多么高兴地摆脱这一切的宏伟

she would have loved to lay aside the heavy wreath!

她很想把沉重的花圈放在一边！
she thought of the red flowers in her own garden
她想起了自己花园里的红色花朵
the red flowers would have suited her much better
红色的花朵会更适合她
But she could not change herself into something else
但她无法把自己变成别的东西
so she said farewell to her grandmother and sisters
于是她告别了祖母和姐妹们
and, as lightly as a bubble, she rose to the surface
然后，她像泡泡一样轻盈地浮出水面

The sun had just set when she raised her head above the waves
当她把头抬到海浪上时，太阳刚刚落山
The clouds were tinted with crimson and gold from the sunset
夕阳下的云彩染上了深红色和金色
and through the glimmering twilight beamed the evening star
透过熠熠生辉的暮色，闪耀着傍晚的星星
The sea was calm, and the sea air was mild and fresh
海面风平浪静，海风温和清新
A large ship with three masts lay becalmed on the water
一艘有三根桅杆的大船平静地躺在水面上
only one sail was set, for not a breeze stirred
只扬起了一面帆，因为没有一丝微风吹动
and the sailors sat idle on deck, or amidst the rigging
水手们闲着坐在甲板上，或坐在索具中
There was music and song on board of the ship
船上有音乐和歌曲
as darkness came a hundred colored lanterns were lighted

夜幕降临，一百盏彩灯被点亮
it was as if the flags of all nations waved in the air
仿佛所有国家的旗帜都在空中飘扬

The little mermaid swam close to the cabin windows
小美人鱼游到靠近机舱窗户的地方
now and then the waves of the sea lifted her up
海浪时不时地把她掀起来
she could look in through the glass window-panes
她可以透过玻璃窗往里看
and she could see a number of curiously dressed people
她可以看到一些穿着奇怪的人
Among the people she could see there was a young prince
在她能看到的人中，有一位年轻的王子
the prince was the most beautiful of them all
王子是他们中最美丽的
she had never seen anyone with such beautiful eyes
她从未见过有如此美丽眼睛的人
it was the celebration of his sixteenth birthday
这是他十六岁生日的庆祝活动
The sailors were dancing on the deck of the ship
水手们在船的甲板上跳舞
all cheered when the prince came out of the cabin
当王子从船舱里出来时，所有人都欢呼起来
and more than a hundred rockets rose into the air
一百多枚火箭升空
for some time the fireworks made the sky as bright as day
有一段时间，烟花使天空像白昼一样明亮
of course our young mermaid had never seen fireworks before
当然，我们年轻的美人鱼以前从未见过烟花

startled by all the noise, she dived back under water
她被所有的噪音吓了一跳,潜回水下

but soon she again stretched out her head
但很快她又伸出了头

it was as if all the stars of heaven were falling around her
仿佛天上所有的星星都落在她周围

splendid fireflies flew up into the blue air
灿烂的萤火虫飞向蓝色的空气

and everything was reflected in the clear, calm sea
一切都倒映在清澈平静的海面上

The ship itself was brightly illuminated by all the light
这艘船本身被所有的光线照亮了

she could see all the people and even the smallest rope
她能看到所有的人,甚至最小的绳子

How handsome the young prince looked thanking his guests!
年轻的王子在感谢他的客人时看起来多么英俊!

and the music resounded through the clear night air!
音乐在晴朗的夜空中回荡!

the birthday celebrations lasted late into the night
生日庆祝活动一直持续到深夜

but the little mermaid could not take her eyes from the ship
但小美人鱼无法将目光从船上移开

nor could she take her eyes from the beautiful prince
她也无法将目光从美丽的王子身上移开

The colored lanterns had now been extinguished
彩色的灯笼现在已经熄灭了

and there were no more rockets that rose into the air
而且没有更多的火箭升到空中

the cannon of the ship had also ceased firing
船上的大炮也停止了射击

but now it was the sea that became restless
但现在是大海变得躁动不安
a moaning, grumbling sound could be heard beneath the waves
在海浪下可以听到呻吟、咕噜咕噜的声音
and yet, the little mermaid remained by the cabin window
然而，小美人鱼仍然留在船舱的窗户旁
she was rocking up and down on the water
她在水面上上下摇晃
so that she could keep looking into the ship
这样她就可以继续看着这艘船
After a while the sails were quickly set
过了一会儿，风帆很快就起航了
and the ship went on her way back to port
这艘船继续返回港口

But soon the waves rose higher and higher
但很快，海浪越涨越高
dark, heavy clouds darkened the night sky
黑暗、厚重的云层使夜空变暗
and there appeared flashes of lightning in the distance
远处出现了闪电
not far away a dreadful storm was approaching
不远处，一场可怕的暴风雨正在逼近
Once more the sails were lowered against the wind
风帆再一次迎风降下
and the great ship pursued her course over the raging sea
这艘大船在汹涌的海面上继续前进
The waves rose as high as the mountains
海浪像山一样高
one would have thought the waves would have had the ship

人们会认为海浪会拥有这艘船
but the ship dived like a swan between the waves
但是这艘船像天鹅一样在海浪之间潜伏
then she rose again on their lofty, foaming crests
然后她又在他们高耸的、泡沫的波峰上站起来
To the little mermaid this was pleasant sport
对小美人鱼来说,这是一项令人愉快的运动
but it was not pleasant sport to the sailors
但这对水手来说并不是一项令人愉快的运动
the ship made awful groaning and creaking sounds
这艘船发出了可怕的呻吟声和吱吱声
and the waves broke over the deck again and again
海浪一次又一次地拍打着甲板
the thick planks gave way under the lashing of the sea
厚厚的木板在海浪的冲击下让位
under the pressure the mainmast snapped asunder, like a reed
在压力下,主桅杆像芦苇一样折断了
and, as the ship lay over on her side, the water rushed in
而且,当船侧躺着时,水冲了进来

The little mermaid realized that the crew were in danger
小美人鱼意识到船员们处于危险之中
her own situation wasn't without danger either
她自己的处境也并非没有危险
she had to avoid the beams and planks scattered in the water
她不得不避开散落在水中的横梁和木板
for a moment everything turned into complete darkness
一时间,一切都变成了完全的黑暗
and the little mermaid could not see where she was

小美人鱼看不见她在哪里
but then a flash of lightning revealed the whole scene
但随后一道闪电揭示了整个场景
she could see everyone was still on board of the ship
她可以看到每个人都还在船上
well, everyone was on board of the ship, except the prince
好吧,除了王子之外,每个人都在船上
the ship continued on its path to the land
这艘船继续前往陆地
and she saw the prince sink into the deep waves
她看到王子沉入深海
for a moment this made her happier than it should have
有那么一会儿,这让她比应该的更快乐
now that he was in the sea she could be with him
现在他在海里,她可以和他在一起
Then she remembered the limits of human beings
然后她想起了人类的局限性
the people of the land cannot live in the water
这片土地上的人民不能生活在水中
if he got to the palace he would already be dead
如果他到了皇宫,他早就死了
"No, he must not die!" she decided
"不,他一定不能死!"她决定
she forget any concern for her own safety
她忘记了对自己安全的担忧
and she swam through the beams and planks
她游过横梁和木板
two beams could easily crush her to pieces
两束光束很容易将她压成碎片
she dove deep under the dark waters
她潜入黑暗的海水深处
everything rose and fell with the waves

一切都随着海浪起伏

finally, she managed to reach the young prince
最后,她设法找到了年轻的王子

he was fast losing the power to swim in the stormy sea
他很快就失去了在波涛汹涌的大海中游泳的能力

His limbs were starting to fail him
他的四肢开始使他失败

and his beautiful eyes were closed
他美丽的眼睛闭上了

he would have died had the little mermaid not come
如果小美人鱼不来,他早就死了

She held his head above the water
她把他的头抬到水面上

and let the waves carry them where they wanted
让海浪把他们带到他们想去的地方

In the morning the storm had ceased
早上,暴风雨停了下来

but of the ship not a single fragment could be seen
但是在船上看不到一个碎片

The sun came up, red and shining, out of the water
太阳从水里升起,红红的,闪闪发光的

the sun's beams had a healing effect on the prince
太阳的光束对王子有治疗作用

the hue of health returned to the prince's cheeks
健康的色调又回到了王子的脸颊上

but despite the sun, his eyes remained closed
但是,尽管有太阳,他的眼睛仍然闭着

The mermaid kissed his high, smooth forehead
美人鱼亲吻了他高高光滑的额头

and she stroked back his wet hair
她抚摸着他湿漉漉的头发

He seemed to her like the marble statue in her garden
在她看来,他就像她花园里的大理石雕像

so she kissed him again, and wished that he lived
于是她又吻了他,希望他能活下去

Presently, they came in sight of land
现在,他们来到了陆地的视线中
and she saw lofty blue mountains on the horizon
她看到地平线上高耸的蓝色山脉
on top of the mountains the white snow rested
山顶上白雪皑皑
as if a flock of swans were lying upon them
仿佛一群天鹅躺在他们身上
Beautiful green forests were near the shore
美丽的绿色森林靠近海岸
and close by there stood a large building
不远处有一座大建筑
it could have been a church or a convent
它可能是一座教堂或修道院
but she was still too far away to be sure
但她离得太远了,无法确定
Orange and citron trees grew in the garden
花园里长着橘子树和香橼树
and before the door stood lofty palms
门前站着高高的棕榈树
The sea here formed a little bay
这里的大海形成了一个小海湾
in the bay the water lay quiet and still
在海湾里,水静静地躺着
but although the water was still, it was very deep
但是虽然水是静止的,但它很深
She swam with the handsome prince to the beach
她和英俊的王子一起游到海滩
the beach was covered with fine white sand
海滩上覆盖着细白的沙滩
and there she laid him in the warm sunshine

她把他放在温暖的阳光下
she took care to raise his head higher than his body
她小心翼翼地把他的头抬得比他的身体还高
Then bells sounded in the large white building
然后钟声在白色的大建筑里响起
some young girls came into the garden
一些年轻女孩走进花园
The little mermaid swam out farther from the shore
小美人鱼游到离岸边更远的地方
she hid herself among some high rocks in the water
她把自己藏在水中的一些高高的岩石中
she Covered her head and neck with the foam of the sea
她用大海的泡沫覆盖了她的头和脖子
and she watched to see what would become of the poor prince
她看着可怜的王子会变成什么样子

It was not long before she saw a young girl approach
没过多久,她就看到一个年轻女孩走了过来
the young girl seemed frightened, at first
起初,这个年轻女孩似乎很害怕
but her fear only lasted for a moment
但她的恐惧只持续了一会儿
then she brought over a number of people
然后她带了几个人过来
and the mermaid saw that the prince came to life again
美人鱼看到王子又活了过来
he smiled upon those who stood around him
他对站在他周围的人微笑
But to the little mermaid the prince sent no smile
但对小美人鱼,王子却没有笑容
he knew not that she had saved him
他不知道她救了他

This made the little mermaid very sorrowful
这让小美人鱼非常悲哀
and then he was led away into the great building
然后他被带到那座伟大的建筑里
and the little mermaid dived down into the water
小美人鱼潜入水中
and she returned to her father's castle
她回到了她父亲的城堡

She had always been the most silent and thoughtful
她一直是最沉默、最体贴的
and now she was more silent and thoughtful than ever
现在她比以往任何时候都更加沉默和深思熟虑
Her sisters asked her what she had seen on her first visit
她的姐妹们问她第一次来访时看到了什么
but she could tell them nothing of what she had seen
但她什么也说不出来
Many an evening and morning she returned to the surface
许多个傍晚和早晨,她都回到了水面
and she went to the place where she had left the prince
她去了她离开王子的地方
She saw the fruits in the garden ripen
她看到花园里的果实成熟了
and she watched the fruits gathered from their trees
她看着从树上摘下来的果子
she watched the snow on the mountain tops melt away
她眼睁睁地看着山顶上的积雪融化
but on none of her visits did she see the prince again
但她没有一次访问再见到王子
and therefore she always returned more sorrowful than before
因此,她总是比以前更悲伤地回来

her only comfort was sitting in her own little garden
她唯一的安慰是坐在自己的小花园里

she flung her arms around the beautiful marble statue
她搂着美丽的大理石雕像

the statue which looked just like the prince
雕像看起来就像王子一样

She had given up tending to her flowers
她已经放弃了照料她的花朵

and her garden grew in wild confusion
她的花园在疯狂的混乱中生长

they twinied their long leaves and stems round the trees
它们将长长的叶子和茎缠绕在树上

so that the whole garden became dark and gloomy
以至于整个花园变得黑暗和阴沉

eventually she could bear it no longer
最终，她再也忍受不了了

and she told one of her sisters all about it
她把这件事告诉了她的一个姐妹

soon the other sisters heard the secret
不久，其他姊妹就听说了这个秘密

and very soon her secret became known to several maids
很快，她的秘密就被几个女仆知道了

one of the maids had a friend who knew about the prince
其中一个女仆有一个朋友知道王子

She had also seen the festival on board the ship
她还在船上看过这个节日

and she told them where the prince came from
她告诉他们王子是从哪里来的

and she told them where his palace stood
她告诉他们他的宫殿在哪里

"Come, little sister," said the other princesses
"来吧,小妹妹," 其他公主说

they entwined their arms and rose up together
他们缠绕着胳膊,一起站了起来

they went near to where the prince's palace stood
他们走到王子宫殿附近

the palace was built of bright-yellow, shining stone
这座宫殿是用亮黄色、闪闪发光的石头建造的

and the palace had long flights of marble steps
宫殿有长长的大理石台阶

one of the flights of steps reached down to the sea
其中一段台阶一直延伸到海边

Splendid gilded cupolas rose over the roof
绚丽的镀金穹顶耸立在屋顶上

the whole building was surrounded by pillars
整个建筑被柱子包围

and between the pillars stood lifelike statues of marble
柱子之间矗立着栩栩如生的大理石雕像

they could see through the clear crystal of the windows
他们能透过窗户的透明水晶看到

and they could look into the noble rooms
他们可以看到高贵的房间

costly silk curtains and tapestries hung from the ceiling
昂贵的丝绸窗帘和挂毯挂在天花板上

and the walls were covered with beautiful paintings
墙上挂满了美丽的画作

In the centre of the largest salon was a fountain
在最大的沙龙的中心是一个喷泉

the fountain threw its sparkling jets high up
喷泉将波光粼粼的喷射器高高抛起

the water splashed onto the glass cupola of the ceiling
水溅到天花板的玻璃穹顶上

and the sun shone in through the water

太阳透过水照进来
and the water splashed on the plants around the fountain
水溅在喷泉周围的植物上

Now the little mermaid knew where the prince lived
现在小美人鱼知道王子住在哪里了
so she spent many a night on those waters
所以她在那些水域上度过了许多夜晚
she got more courageous than her sisters had been
她变得比她的姐妹们更勇敢
and she swam much nearer the shore than they had
她游得比他们更靠近岸边
once she went up the narrow channel, under the marble balcony
有一次,她走上狭窄的通道,在大理石阳台下
the balcony threw a broad shadow on the water
阳台在水面上投下了宽阔的阴影
Here she sat and watched the young prince
她坐在这里,看着年轻的王子
he, of course, thought he was alone in the bright moonlight
当然,他以为自己一个人在明亮的月光下

She often saw him evenings, sailing in a beautiful boat
她经常在晚上看到他,在一艘美丽的船上航行
music sounded from the boat and the flags waved
音乐从船上响起,旗帜飘扬
She peeped out from among the green rushes
她从绿色的草丛中探出头来
at times the wind caught her long silvery-white veil
有时,风吹过她长长的银白色面纱
those who saw it believed it to be a swan
看到它的人认为它是一只天鹅

it had all the appearance of a swan spreading its wings
它看起来像一只张开翅膀的天鹅

Many a night, too, she watched the fishermen set their nets
许多个晚上,她也看着渔民撒网

they cast their nets in the light of their torches
他们在火把的光下撒网

and she heard them tell many good things about the prince
她听见他们说了很多关于王子的好话

this made her glad that she had saved his life
这让她庆幸自己救了他的命

when he was tossed around half dead on the waves
当他被抛在海浪上半死不活时

She remembered how his head had rested on her bosom
她记得他的头是如何靠在她的怀里的

and she remembered how heartily she had kissed him
她记得她曾经多么衷心地吻过他

but he knew nothing of all that had happened
但他对所发生的一切一无所知

the young prince could not even dream of the little mermaid
年轻的王子甚至做梦也想不到小美人鱼

She grew to like human beings more and more
她越来越喜欢人类

she wished more and more to be able to wander their world
她越来越希望能够在他们的世界里徘徊

their world seemed to be so much larger than her own
他们的世界似乎比她自己的世界大得多

They could fly over the sea in ships

他们可以乘船飞越大海

and they could mount the high hills far above the clouds
他们可以登上远高于云层的高山

in their lands they possessed woods and fields
在他们的土地上,他们拥有树林和田野

the greenery stretched beyond the reach of her sight
绿色植物延伸到她视线之外

There was so much that she wished to know!
她想知道的太多了!

but her sisters were unable to answer all her questions
但她的姐妹们无法回答她所有的问题

She then went to her old grandmother for answers
然后她去找她的老祖母寻求答案

her grandmother knew all about the upper world
她的祖母对上层世界了如指掌

she rightly called this world "the lands above the sea"
她正确地称这个世界为"海上之地"

"If human beings are not drowned, can they live forever?"
"如果人类没有被淹死,他们还能长生不老吗?"

"Do they never die, as we do here in the sea?"
"难道它们永远不会死,就像我们在海里一样吗?"

"Yes, they die too" replied the old lady
"是的,他们也死了," 老太太回答说

"like us, they must also die," added her grandmother
"像我们一样,他们也必须死," 她的祖母补充道

"and their lives are even shorter than ours"
"他们的生命甚至比我们短"

"We sometimes live for three hundred years"
"我们有时能活三百年"

"but when we cease to exist here we become foam"
"但当我们在这里不复存在时,我们就会变成泡沫"

"and we float on the surface of the water"
"我们漂浮在水面上"

"we do not have graves for those we love"
"我们没有为我们所爱的人建立坟墓"

"and we have not immortal souls"
"我们没有不朽的灵魂"

"after we die we shall never live again"
"我们死后再也不会活了"

"like the green seaweed, once it has been cut off"
"就像绿色的海藻一样，一旦被切断"

"after we die, we can never flourish more"
"我们死后，再也无法繁衍生息"

"Human beings, on the contrary, have souls"
"相反，人类有灵魂"

"even after they're dead their souls live forever"
"即使他们死了，他们的灵魂也永远活着"

"when we die our bodies turn to foam"
"当我们死去时，我们的身体会变成泡沫"

"when they die their bodies turn to dust"
"当他们死去时，他们的身体会化为尘土"

"when we die we rise through the clear, blue water"
"当我们死去时，我们会从清澈湛蓝的水中升起"

"when they die they rise up through the clear, pure air"
"当他们死去时，他们会在清澈、纯净的空气中升起"

"when we die we float no further than the surface"
"当我们死去时，我们漂浮在水面上"

"but when they die they go beyond the glittering stars"
"但当他们死去时，他们超越了闪闪发光的星星"

"we rise out of the water to the surface"
"我们从水里浮出水面"

"and we behold all the land of the earth"
"我们看见地上全地"

"they rise to unknown and glorious regions"
"他们上升到未知和光荣的地区"

"glorious and unknown regions which we shall never see"
　"我们永远看不到的光荣和未知的地区"
the little mermaid mourned her lack of a soul
小美人鱼哀悼她没有灵魂
"Why have not we immortal souls?" asked the little mermaid
　"为什么我们没有不朽的灵魂？" 小美人鱼问道
"I would gladly give all the hundreds of years that I have"
　"我很乐意奉献我所拥有的数百年"
"I would trade it all to be a human being for one day"
　"我愿意用这一切来换取一天的人类"
"to have the hope of knowing such happiness"
　"有希望知道这样的幸福"
"the happiness of that glorious world above the stars"
　"星空之上那个光荣世界的幸福"
"You must not think that," said the old woman
　"你千万不要这么想，" 老妇人说
"We believe that we are much happier than the humans"
　"我们相信我们比人类快乐得多"
"and we believe we are much better off than human beings"
　"我们相信我们比人类过得好得多"

"So I shall die," said the little mermaid
　"所以我会死的，" 小美人鱼说
"being the foam of the sea, I shall be washed about"
　"我是大海的泡沫，我将被冲走"
"never again will I hear the music of the waves"
　"我再也不会听到海浪的音乐了"
"never again will I see the pretty flowers"
　"我再也见不到美丽的花朵了"

"nor will I ever again see the red sun"
"我也再也见不到红日了"

"Is there anything I can do to win an immortal soul?"
"我能做些什么来赢得一个不朽的灵魂吗？"

"No," said the old woman, "unless..."
"不，"老妇人说，"除非……"

"there is just one way to gain a soul"
"只有一种方法可以获得灵魂"

"a man has to love you more than he loves his father and mother"
"一个男人必须爱你胜过爱他的父亲和母亲"

"all his thoughts and love must be fixed upon you"
"他所有的思想和爱都必须固定在你身上"

"he has to promise to be true to you here and hereafter"
"他必须应许今生和来世对你忠心耿耿"

"the priest has to place his right hand in yours"
"牧师必须把他的右手放在你的手上"

"then your man's soul would glide into your body"
"然后你男人的灵魂会滑入你的身体"

"you would get a share in the future happiness of mankind"
"你会分享人类未来的幸福"

"He would give to you a soul and retain his own as well"
"他会给你一个灵魂，也保留他自己的灵魂"

"but it is impossible for this to ever happen"
"但这是不可能的"

"Your fish's tail, among us, is considered beautiful"
"你的鱼尾巴，在我们中间，被认为是美丽的"

"but on earth your fish's tail is considered ugly"
"但到底你的鱼尾巴被认为是丑陋的"

"The humans do not know any better"
"人类再清楚不过了"

"their standard of beauty is having two stout props"

"他们的美的标准是拥有两个粗壮的道具"
"these two stout props they call their legs"
"这两个粗壮的道具,他们称之为腿"

The little mermaid sighed at what appeared to be her destiny
小美人鱼叹了口气,这似乎是她的命运

and she looked sorrowfully at her fish's tail
她悲伤地看着她的鱼尾巴

"Let us be happy with what we have," said the old lady
"让我们对我们所拥有的感到满意," 老太太说

"let us dart and spring about for the three hundred years"
"让我们飞镖和春天三百年"

"and three hundred years really is quite long enough"
"三百年真的足够长了"

"After that we can rest ourselves all the better"
"在那之后,我们可以更好地休息"

"This evening we are going to have a court ball"
"今晚我们要举行一场宫廷舞会"

It was one of those splendid sights we can never see on earth
这是我们在地球上永远看不到的壮丽景象之一

the court ball took place in a large ballroom
法庭舞会在一个大宴会厅举行

The walls and the ceiling were of thick transparent crystal
墙壁和天花板是厚厚的透明水晶

Many hundreds of colossal shells stood in rows on each side
数百个巨大的炮弹在两侧排成一排

some were deep red, others were grass green
有些是深红色的,有些是草绿色的

and each of the shells had a blue fire in it

每个炮弹里都有蓝色的火焰
These lighted up the whole salon and the dancers
这些点亮了整个沙龙和舞者
and the shells shone out through the walls
贝壳透过墙壁闪耀
so that the sea was also illuminated by their light
因此,大海也被他们的光芒照亮了
Innumerable fishes, great and small, swam past
无数大大小小的鱼游过
some of their scales glowed with a purple brilliance
他们的一些鳞片闪耀着紫色的光辉
and other fishes shone like silver and gold
其他鱼像金银一样闪闪发光
Through the halls flowed a broad stream
大厅里流淌着一条宽阔的溪流
and in the stream danced the mermen and the mermaids
在溪流中跳舞的人鱼和美人鱼
they danced to the music of their own sweet singing
他们随着自己甜美的歌声跳舞

No one on earth has such lovely voices as they
地球上没有人像他们一样拥有如此可爱的声音
but the little mermaid sang more sweetly than all
但小美人鱼唱得比所有人都甜美
The whole court applauded her with hands and tails
整个球场都为她鼓掌
and for a moment her heart felt quite happy
有那么一会儿,她的心里感到非常高兴
because she knew she had the sweetest voice in the sea
因为她知道自己拥有大海中最甜美的声音
and she knew she had the sweetest voice on land
她知道自己拥有陆地上最甜美的声音
But soon she thought again of the world above her

但很快，她又想到了她头顶的世界
she could not forget the charming prince
她忘不了那位迷人的王子
it reminded her that he had an immortal soul
这让她想起了他有一个不朽的灵魂
and she could not forget that she had no immortal soul
她不能忘记，她没有不朽的灵魂
She crept away silently out of her father's palace
她悄无声息地离开了她父亲的宫殿
everything within was full of gladness and song
里面的一切都充满了喜悦和歌声
but she sat in her own little garden, sorrowful and alone
但她坐在自己的小花园里，悲伤而孤独
Then she heard the bugle sounding through the water
然后她听到号角在水中响起
and she thought, "He is certainly sailing above"
她想，"他肯定在上面航行"
"he, the beautiful prince, in whom my wishes centre"
"他，美丽的王子，我的愿望集中在他身上"
"he, in whose hands I should like to place my happiness"
"他，我想把我的幸福交到他手中"
"I will venture all for him, and to win an immortal soul"
"我会为他冒险，赢得一个不朽的灵魂"
"my sisters are dancing in my father's palace"
"我的姐妹们在我父亲的宫殿里跳舞"
"but I will go to the sea witch"
"但我会去找海女巫"
"the sea witch of whom I have always been so afraid"
"我一直很害怕的海女巫"
"but the sea witch can give me counsel, and help"
"但海女巫可以给我忠告和帮助"

Then the little mermaid went out from her garden
然后小美人鱼从她的花园里走了出来
and she took the road to the foaming whirlpools
她走上了通往泡沫漩涡的道路
behind the foaming whirlpools the sorceress lived
在起泡的漩涡后面,女巫住着
the little mermaid had never gone that way before
小美人鱼以前从未走过这条路
Neither flowers nor grass grew where she was going
她要去的地方既不长花也不长草
there was nothing but bare, gray, sandy ground
除了光秃秃的、灰色的、沙质的地面,什么都没有
this barren land stretched out to the whirlpool
这片贫瘠的土地一直延伸到漩涡
the water was like foaming mill wheels
水就像起泡的磨轮
and the mills seized everything that came within reach
磨坊抓住了一切触手可及的东西
they cast their prey into the fathomless deep
他们把猎物扔进深不可测的深渊
Through these crushing whirlpools she had to pass
穿过这些压碎的漩涡,她必须通过
only then could she reach the dominions of the sea witch
只有这样,她才能到达海女巫的领地
after this came a stretch of warm, bubbling mire
在这之后是一段温暖的、冒泡的泥潭
the sea witch called the bubbling mire her turf moor
海女巫称冒泡的泥潭是她的地盘沼泽地

Beyond her turf moor was the witch's house
在她的草皮沼泽地之外是女巫的房子
her house stood in the centre of a strange forest
她的房子矗立在一片陌生的森林的中心

in this forest all the trees and flowers were polypi
在这片森林里,所有的树木和花朵都是息里虫
but they were only half plant; the other half was animal
但它们只是半株植物;另一半是动物
They looked like serpents with a hundred heads
他们看起来像有一百个头的蛇
and each serpent was growing out of the ground
每条蛇都从地里长出来
Their branches were long, slimy arms
它们的树枝是长而粘稠的手臂
and they had fingers like flexible worms
他们的手指像灵活的蠕虫
each of their limbs, from the root to the top, moved
他们的每一个肢体,从根部到顶部,都在移动
All that could be reached in the sea they seized upon
他们所抓住的海中所能到达的一切
and what they caught they held on tightly to
他们抓住了什么,他们紧紧抓住
so that it never escaped from their clutches
这样它就再也逃不出他们的魔掌

The little mermaid was alarmed at what she saw
小美人鱼被她所看到的景象吓了一跳
she stood still and her heart beat with fear
她站着不动,心因恐惧而跳动
She came very close to turning back
她差点回头
but she thought of the beautiful prince
但她想到了美丽的王子
and the thought of the human soul for which she longed
以及她渴望的人类灵魂的想法
with these thoughts her courage returned

有了这些想法，她的勇气又回来了
She fastened her long, flowing hair round her head
她把飘逸的长发系在头上
so that the polypi could not grab hold of her hair
这样息肉就无法抓住她的头发
and she crossed her hands across her bosom
她双手交叉在胸前
and then she darted forward like a fish through the water
然后她像鱼一样在水中向前冲
between the supple arms and fingers of the ugly polypi
在丑陋的波利皮柔软的手臂和手指之间
they were stretched out on each side of her
它们在她的两侧伸展
She saw that they all held something in their grasp
她看到他们都手里拿着什么东西
something they had seized with their numerous little arms
他们用无数的小胳膊抓住了什么
they were were white skeletons of human beings
他们是人类的白色骷髅
sailors who had perished at sea in storms
在暴风雨中丧生的水手
and they had sunk down into the deep waters
他们沉入深水区
and there were skeletons of land animals
还有陆地动物的骨架
and there were oars, rudders, and chests of ships
还有桨、舵和船箱
There was even a little mermaid whom they had caught
甚至还有一条小美人鱼被他们抓到的
the poor mermaid must have been strangled by the

hands
可怜的美人鱼一定是被双手勒死了
to her this seemed the most shocking of all
对她来说，这似乎是最令人震惊的

finally, she came to a space of marshy ground in the woods
最后，她来到了树林里的一片沼泽地
here there were large fat water snakes rolling in the mire
这里有大胖水蛇在泥潭里打滚
the snakes showed their ugly, drab-colored bodies
蛇露出了丑陋、单调的身体
In the midst of this spot stood a house
在这个地方中间矗立着一座房子
the house was built of the bones of shipwrecked human beings
这座房子是用遇难者的骨头建造的
and in the house sat the sea witch
屋子里坐着海女巫
she was allowing a toad to eat from her mouth
她让一只蟾蜍从她的嘴里吃东西
just like when people feed a canary with pieces of sugar
就像人们用糖片喂金丝雀一样
She called the ugly water snakes her little chickens
她称丑陋的水蛇为她的小鸡
and she allowed them to crawl all over her bosom
她允许它们爬到她的怀里

"I know what you want," said the sea witch
"我知道你想要什么，" 海女巫说
"It is very stupid of you to want such a thing"
"你想要这样的东西是很愚蠢的"

"but you shall have your way, however stupid it is"
 "但你要走你的路,不管它有多愚蠢"

"though it will bring you to sorrow, my pretty princess"
 "虽然它会让你悲伤,我美丽的公主"

"You want to get rid of your mermaid's tail"
 "你想摆脱你的美人鱼尾巴"

"and you want to have two supports instead"
 "而你希望有两个支撑"

"this will make you like the human beings on earth"
 "这会让你像地球上的人类一样"

"and then the young prince might fall in love with you"
 "然后小王子可能会爱上你"

"and then you might have an immortal soul"
 "然后你可能会有一个不朽的灵魂"

the witch laughed loud and disgustingly
女巫大声笑了起来,令人作呕

the toad and the snakes fell to the ground
蟾蜍和蛇倒在地上

and they lay there wriggling on the floor
他们躺在地板上蠕动

"You are but just in time," said the witch
 "你来得正是时候," 女巫说

"after sunrise tomorrow it would have been too late"
 "明天日出之后就太晚了"

"I would not be able to help you till the end of another year"
 "再过一年,我就帮不了你了"

"I will prepare a potion for you"
 "我给你准备药水"

"swim up to the land tomorrow, before sunrise
 "明天在日出之前游到陆地上

"seat yourself there and drink the potion"

"坐在那里喝药水"

"after you drink it your tail will disappear"
"喝完后,你的尾巴就会消失"

"and then you will have what men call legs"
"然后你就会有男人所说的腿"

"all will say you are the prettiest girl in the world"
"所有人都会说你是世界上最漂亮的女孩"

"but for this you will have to endure great pain"
"但为此,你将不得不忍受巨大的痛苦"

"it will be as if a sword were passing through you"
"就好像一把剑从你身上穿过"

"You will still have the same gracefulness of movement"
"你仍然会有同样优雅的动作"

"it will be as if you are floating over the ground"
"就好像你漂浮在地面上一样"

"and no dancer will ever tread as lightly as you"
"没有一个舞者会像你一样轻盈"

"but every step you take will cause you great pain"
"但你走的每一步都会给你带来巨大的痛苦"

"it will be as if you were treading upon sharp knives"
"就好像你踩在锋利的刀子上一样"

"If you bear all this suffering, I will help you"
"如果你承受这一切痛苦,我会帮助你"

the little mermaid thought of the prince
小美人鱼想到了王子

and she thought of the happiness of an immortal soul
她想到了一个不朽灵魂的幸福

"Yes, I will," said the little princess
"是的,我会的,"小公主说

but, as you can imagine, her voice trembled with fear
但是,正如你可以想象的那样,她的声音因恐惧而颤抖

"do not rush into this," said the witch
"不要急于求成，"女巫说

"once you are shaped like a human, you can never return"
"一旦你被塑造成人类，你就再也回不来了"

"and you will never again take the form of a mermaid"
"你再也不会变成美人鱼了"

"You will never return through the water to your sisters"
"你永远不会通过水回到你的姐妹身边"

"nor will you ever go to your father's palace again"
"你也不会再去你父亲的宫殿了"

"you will have to win the love of the prince"
"你必须赢得王子的爱"

"he must be willing to forget his father and mother for you"
"他一定愿意为你忘记他的父母"

"and he must love you with all of his soul"
"他必须全心全意地爱你"

"the priest must join your hands together"
"神父必须把你们的手合在一起"

"and he must make you man and wife in holy matrimony"
"他必须使你们成为圣洁婚姻中的夫妻"

"only then will you have an immortal soul"
"只有这样，你才会拥有不朽的灵魂"

"but you must never allow him to marry another"
"但你绝不能让他娶别人"

"the morning after he marries another, your heart will break"
"他娶了别人的第二天早上，你的心会碎"

"and you will become foam on the crest of the waves"
"你会成为波峰上的泡沫"

the little mermaid became as pale as death

小美人鱼变得像死亡一样苍白

"I will do it," said the little mermaid
"我会做的,"小美人鱼说

"But I must be paid, also," said the witch
"但我也必须得到报酬,"女巫说

"and it is not a trifle that I ask for"
"这不是我要求的小事"

"You have the sweetest voice of any who dwell here"
"你拥有所有住在这里的人中最甜美的声音"

"you believe that you can charm the prince with your voice"
"你相信你可以用你的声音迷住王子"

"But your beautiful voice you must give to me"
"但你美丽的声音,你必须给我"

"The best thing you possess is the price of my potion"
"你拥有的最好的东西就是我的魔药价格"

"the potion must be mixed with my own blood"
"药水必须与我自己的血液混合"

"only this makes it as sharp as a two-edged sword"
"只有这样,它才能像一把双刃剑一样锋利"

the little mermaid tried to object to the cost
小美人鱼试图反对这个代价

"But if you take away my voice..." said the little mermaid
"但如果你夺走我的声音……"小美人鱼说

"if you take away my voice, what is left for me?"
"如果你夺走了我的声音,我还剩下什么?"

"Your beautiful form," suggested the sea witch
"你美丽的身躯,"海女巫建议道

"your graceful walk, and your expressive eyes"
"你优雅的走路,和你富有表现力的眼睛"

"Surely, with these you can enchain a man's heart?"

"当然，有了这些，你就能枷锁一个人的心吗？"

"Well, have you lost your courage?" the sea witch asked
"嗯，你失去勇气了吗？"海女巫问道

"Put out your little tongue, so that I can cut it off"
"把你的小舌头伸出来，这样我就可以把它割掉了"

"then you shall have the powerful potion"
"那你就有了强大的药水"

"It shall be," said the little mermaid
小人鱼说："就这样吧"

Then the witch placed her caldron on the fire
然后女巫把她的火炉放在火上

"Cleanliness is a good thing," said the sea witch
"清洁是一件好事，"海女巫说

she scoured the vessels for the right snake
她在船只中搜寻合适的蛇

all the snakes had been tied together in a large knot
所有的蛇都被打成一个大结

Then she pricked herself in the breast
然后她刺了自己的胸膛

and she let the black blood drop into the caldron
她让黑色的血液滴进火山口

The steam that rose twisted itself into horrible shapes
升起的蒸汽扭曲成可怕的形状

no person could look at the shapes without fear
没有人能无所畏惧地看着这些形状

Every moment the witch threw new ingredients into the vessel
女巫每时每刻都会将新的食材扔进容器中

finally, with everything inside, the caldron began to boil
最后，所有东西都装在里面，火山口开始沸腾

there was the sound like the weeping of a crocodile
有鳄鱼哭泣的声音

and at last the magic potion was ready
魔法药水终于准备好了

despite its ingredients, it looked like the clearest water
尽管它的成分，它看起来像是最清澈的水

"There it is, all for you," said the witch
"就是这样，一切都是为了你，"女巫说

and then she cut off the little mermaid's tongue
然后她割掉了小美人鱼的舌头

so that the little mermaid could never again speak, nor sing
这样小美人鱼就再也不能说话了，也再也不能唱歌了

"the polypi might try and grab you on the way out"
"波利皮可能会试图在离开的路上抓住你"

"if they try, throw over them a few drops of the potion"
"如果他们尝试，就把几滴药水扔在他们身上"

"and their fingers will be torn into a thousand pieces"
"他们的手指将被撕成一千块"

But the little mermaid had no need to do this
但小美人鱼没有必要这样做

the polypi sprang back in terror when they saw her
当波利皮人看到她时，他们惊恐地跳了起来

they saw she had lost her tongue to the sea witch
他们看到她已经失去了对海女巫的舌头

and they saw she was carrying the potion
他们看到她拿着药水

the potion shone in her hand like a twinkling star
药水在她手中闪闪发光，就像一颗闪烁的星星

So she passed quickly through the wood and the marsh
于是她迅速穿过树林和沼泽地

and she passed between the rushing whirlpools
她在奔腾的漩涡之间经过

soon she made it back to the palace of her father
不久，她回到了她父亲的宫殿

all the torches in the ballroom were extinguished
宴会厅里所有的火把都熄灭了
all within the palace must now be asleep
宫殿里的人现在一定都睡着了
But she did not go inside to see them
但她没有进去看他们
she knew she was going to leave them forever
她知道她将永远离开他们
and she knew her heart would break if she saw them
她知道，如果她看到他们，她的心会碎
she went into the garden one last time
她最后一次走进花园
and she took a flower from each one of her sisters
她从她的每个姐妹那里拿了一朵花
and then she rose up through the dark-blue waters
然后她从深蓝色的海水中升起

the little mermaid arrived at the prince's palace
小美人鱼来到了王子的宫殿
the the sun had not yet risen from the sea
太阳还没有从海里升起
and the moon shone clear and bright in the night
月亮在夜里闪耀着清澈明亮的光芒
the little mermaid sat at the beautiful marble steps
小美人鱼坐在美丽的大理石台阶上
and then the little mermaid drank the magic potion
然后小美人鱼喝下了魔法药水
she felt the cut of a two-edged sword cut through her
她感觉到一把双刃剑的刀切开了她
and she fell into a swoon, and lay like one dead
她昏迷不醒，像死人一样躺着
the sun rose from the sea and shone over the land
太阳从海中升起，照耀着大地
she recovered and felt the pain from the cut

她恢复了过来，感觉到割伤的疼痛
but before her stood the handsome young prince
但站在她面前的是英俊的年轻王子

He fixed his coal-black eyes upon the little mermaid
他用煤黑色的眼睛盯着小美人鱼
he looked so earnestly that she cast down her eyes
他如此认真地看着她，以至于她垂下了眼睛
and then she became aware that her fish's tail was gone
然后她意识到她的鱼尾巴不见了
she saw that she had the prettiest pair of white legs
她看到她有一双最漂亮的白腿
and she had tiny feet, as any little maiden would have
她有一双小脚，就像任何小姑娘一样
But, having come from the sea, she had no clothes
但是，她从海里来，没有衣服
so she wrapped herself in her long, thick hair
于是她把自己裹在又长又浓的头发里
The prince asked her who she was and whence she came
王子问她是谁，从哪里来的
She looked at him mildly and sorrowfully
她温和而悲伤地看着他
but she had to answer with her deep blue eyes
但她不得不用她深蓝色的眼睛回答
because the little mermaid could not speak anymore
因为小美人鱼再也说不出话来了
He took her by the hand and led her to the palace
他拉着她的手，把她带到了宫殿里

Every step she took was as the witch had said it would be
她迈出的每一步都像女巫所说的那样
she felt as if she were treading upon sharp knives

她觉得自己好像踩在锋利的刀子上
She bore the pain of the spell willingly, however
然而,她心甘情愿地承受着咒语的痛苦
and she moved at the prince's side as lightly as a bubble
她像泡泡一样轻盈地在王子身边移动
all who saw her wondered at her graceful, swaying movements
所有看到她的人都惊叹于她优雅、摇曳的动作
She was very soon arrayed in costly robes of silk and muslin
很快,她就穿上了昂贵的丝绸和细布长袍
and she was the most beautiful creature in the palace
她是宫殿里最美丽的生物
but she appeared dumb, and could neither speak nor sing
但她看起来很哑,既不能说话,也不能唱歌

there were beautiful female slaves, dressed in silk and gold
有美丽的女奴隶,穿着丝绸和黄金
they stepped forward and sang in front of the royal family
他们走上前去,在王室面前唱歌
each slave could sing better than the next one
每个奴隶都可以比下一个奴隶唱得更好
and the prince clapped his hands and smiled at her
王子拍了拍手,对她微笑
This was a great sorrow to the little mermaid
这对小美人鱼来说是一个巨大的悲哀
she knew how much more sweetly she was able to sing
她知道自己能唱得多么甜美
"if only he knew I have given away my voice to be with him!"

"要是他知道我放弃了我的声音和他在一起就好了!"

there was music being played by an orchestra
管弦乐队正在演奏音乐
and the slaves performed some pretty, fairy-like dances
奴隶们表演了一些漂亮的、仙女般的舞蹈
Then the little mermaid raised her lovely white arms
然后小美人鱼举起了她可爱的白皙手臂
she stood on the tips of her toes like a ballerina
她像芭蕾舞演员一样踮起脚尖
and she glided over the floor like a bird over water
她像鸟儿在水面上一样在地板上滑行
and she danced as no one yet had been able to dance
她跳舞,因为还没有人会跳舞
At each moment her beauty was more revealed
每时每刻,她的美丽都更加显露
most appealing of all, to the heart, were her expressive eyes
最吸引人的是她富有表现力的眼睛
Everyone was enchanted by her, especially the prince
每个人都被她迷住了,尤其是王子
the prince called her his deaf little foundling
王子称她为聋哑小弃儿
and she happily continued to dance, to please the prince
她高兴地继续跳舞,以取悦王子
but we must remember the pain she endured for his pleasure
但我们必须记住她为他的快乐而忍受的痛苦
every step on the floor felt as if she trod on sharp knives
在地板上的每一步都感觉自己踩在锋利的刀子上

The prince said she should remain with him always
王子说她应该永远和他在一起
and she was given permission to sleep at his door
她被允许睡在他家门口
they brought a velvet cushion for her to lie on
他们给她带来了一个天鹅绒垫子,让她躺在上面
and the prince had a page's dress made for her
王子为她做了一件佩奇的裙子
this way she could accompany him on horseback
这样她就可以陪他骑马了
They rode together through the sweet-scented woods
他们一起骑马穿过芬芳的树林
in the woods the green branches touched their shoulders
在树林里,绿色的树枝碰到了他们的肩膀
and the little birds sang among the fresh leaves
小鸟儿在新鲜的树叶中歌唱
She climbed with him to the tops of high mountains
她和他一起爬上了高山的顶端
and although her tender feet bled, she only smiled
虽然她嫩嫩的脚流血了,但她只是笑了笑
she followed him till the clouds were beneath them
她跟着他,直到乌云在他们脚下
like a flock of birds flying to distant lands
像一群飞向遥远国度的鸟儿

when all were asleep she sat on the broad marble steps
当所有人都睡着了时,她坐在宽阔的大理石台阶上
it eased her burning feet to bathe them in the cold water
它缓解了她灼热的脚,让它们沐浴在冷水中
It was then that she thought of all those in the sea
就在那时,她想到了海里的所有人
Once, during the night, her sisters came up, arm in arm

有一次，在夜里，她的姐妹们手挽手走了过来

they sang sorrowfully as they floated on the water
他们漂浮在水面上时悲伤地唱着歌

She beckoned to them, and they recognized her
她向他们招手，他们认出了她

they told her how they had grieved their youngest sister
他们告诉她，他们是如何为他们最小的妹妹感到悲伤的

after that, they came to the same place every night
在那之后，他们每天晚上都来到同一个地方

Once she saw in the distance her old grandmother
有一次，她在远处看到她的老祖母

she had not been to the surface of the sea for many years
她已经很多年没有去过海面了

and the old Sea King, her father, with his crown on his head
还有老海王，她的父亲，头上戴着王冠

he too came to where she could see him
他也来到了她能看到他的地方

They stretched out their hands towards her
他们向她伸出双手

but they did not venture as near the land as her sisters
但她们并没有像她的姐妹们那样冒险靠近这片土地

As the days passed she loved the prince more dearly
随着时间的流逝，她更加深爱着王子

and he loved her as one would love a little child
他爱她，就像爱一个小孩子一样

The thought never came to him to make her his wife
他从未想过要让她成为他的妻子

but, unless he married her, her wish would never come true
但是，除非他娶了她，否则她的愿望永远不会实现

unless he married her she could not receive an immortal soul
除非他娶了她,否则她无法得到不朽的灵魂

and if he married another her dreams would shatter
如果他娶了另一个人,她的梦想就会破灭

on the morning after his marriage she would dissolve
在他结婚后的第二天早上,她会解散

and the little mermaid would become the foam of the sea
小美人鱼会变成大海的泡沫

the prince took the little mermaid in his arms
王子把小美人鱼抱在怀里

and he kissed her on her forehead
他吻了吻她的额头

with her eyes she tried to ask him
她用眼睛试图问他

"Do you not love me the most of them all?"
"你不是最爱我吗?"

"Yes, you are dear to me," said the prince
"是的,你是我的宝贝,"王子说

"because you have the best heart"
"因为你有最好的心"

"and you are the most devoted to me"
"而你是对我最忠诚的"

"You are like a young maiden whom I once saw"
"你就像我曾经见过的年轻少女"

"but I shall never meet this young maiden again"
"但我再也见不到这个年轻的少女了"

"I was in a ship that was wrecked"
"我在一艘失事的船上"

"and the waves cast me ashore near a holy temple"
"海浪把我扔到圣殿附近的岸上"

"at the temple several young maidens performed the

service"
"在圣殿里，有几位年轻的少女主持了礼拜"

"The youngest maiden found me on the shore"
"最小的少女在岸上找到了我"

"and the youngest of the maidens saved my life"
"最小的少女救了我的命"

"I saw her but twice," he explained
"我见过她两次，"他解释道

"and she is the only one in the world whom I could love"
"她是世界上唯一一个我能爱的人"

"But you are like her," he reassured the little mermaid
"但你和她一样，"他向小美人鱼保证

"and you have almost driven her image from my mind"
"你几乎把她的形象从我的脑海中赶走了"

"She belongs to the holy temple"
"她属于圣殿"

"good fortune has sent you instead of her to me"
"好运把你而不是她送到我这里"

"We will never part," he comforted the little mermaid
"我们永远不会分开，"他安慰小美人鱼

but the little mermaid could not help but sigh
小美人鱼却忍不住叹了口气

"he knows not that it was I who saved his life"
"他不知道是我救了他的命"

"I carried him over the sea to where the temple stands"
"我把他带到海边，来到圣殿所在的地方"

"I sat beneath the foam till the human came to help him"
"我坐在泡沫下面，直到人类来帮助他"

"I saw the pretty maiden that he loves"
"我看到了他所爱的漂亮少女"

"the pretty maiden that he loves more than me"

"他爱得比我还多的漂亮少女"

The mermaid sighed deeply, but she could not weep
美人鱼深深地叹了口气,却哭不出来

"He says the maiden belongs to the holy temple"
"他说少女属于圣殿"

"therefore she will never return to the world"
"因此,她永远不会回到这个世界"

"they will meet no more," the little mermaid hoped
"他们不会再见面了,"小美人鱼希望

"I am by his side and see him every day"
"我在他身边,每天都能见到他"

"I will take care of him, and love him"
"我会照顾他,爱他"

"and I will give up my life for his sake"
"我愿意为他放弃我的生命"

Very soon it was said that the prince was to marry
不久,据说王子要结婚了

there was the beautiful daughter of a neighbouring king
有一个邻近国王的美丽女儿

it was said that she would be his wife
据说她会成为他的妻子

for the occasion a fine ship was being fitted out
为此,一艘精美的船正在装修中

the prince said he intended only to visit the king
王子说他只打算去拜访国王

they thought he was only going so as to meet the princess
他们以为他只是为了见公主而去的

The little mermaid smiled and shook her head
小美人鱼笑着摇了摇头

She knew the prince's thoughts better than the others
她比其他人更了解王子的想法

"I must travel," he had said to her
"我必须去旅行," 他对她说

"I must see this beautiful princess"
"我必须见到这位美丽的公主"

"My parents want me to go and see her
"我的父母希望我去看她

"but they will not oblige me to bring her home as my bride"
"但他们不会强迫我把她带回家做我的新娘"

"you know that I cannot love her"
"你知道我不能爱她"

"because she is not like the beautiful maiden in the temple"
"因为她不像寺庙里的美少女"

"the beautiful maiden whom you resemble"
"你喜欢的美丽少女"

"If I were forced to choose a bride, I would choose you"
"如果让我选择新娘,我会选择你"

"my deaf foundling, with those expressive eyes"
"我的聋哑弃儿,用那双富有表现力的眼睛"

Then he kissed her rosy mouth
然后他吻了她红润的嘴

and he played with her long, waving hair
他把玩着她飘扬的长发

and he laid his head on her heart
他把头放在她的心上

she dreamed of human happiness and an immortal soul
她梦想着人类的幸福和不朽的灵魂

they stood on the deck of the noble ship
他们站在贵族船的甲板上

"You are not afraid of the sea, are you?" he said
"你不怕海,是吗?" 他说

the ship was to carry them to the neighbouring country
这艘船将把他们带到邻国

Then he told her of storms and of calms
然后他告诉她暴风雨和平静

he told her of strange fishes deep beneath the water
他告诉她水底深处有奇怪的鱼

and he told her of what the divers had seen there
他告诉她潜水员在那里看到了什么

She smiled at his descriptions, slightly amused
她对他的描述笑了笑，有点好笑

she knew better what wonders were at the bottom of the sea
她更清楚海底有什么奇观

the little mermaid sat on the deck at moonlight
小美人鱼在月光下坐在甲板上

all on board were asleep, except the man at the helm
船上的所有人都睡着了，除了掌舵的人

and she gazed down through the clear water
她透过清澈的海水向下凝视

She thought she could distinguish her father's castle
她以为她能分辨出她父亲的城堡

and in the castle she could see her aged grandmother
在城堡里，她可以看到她年迈的祖母

Then her sisters came out of the waves
然后她的姐妹们从海浪中出来了

and they gazed at their sister mournfully
他们悲哀地凝视着他们的妹妹

She beckoned to her sisters, and smiled
她向她的姐妹们招了招手，微笑着

she wanted to tell them how happy and well off she was
她想告诉他们她是多么的幸福和富裕

But the cabin boy approached and her sisters dived

down
但是机舱男孩走近了,她的姐妹们潜了下去

he thought what he saw was the foam of the sea
他以为他看到的是大海的泡沫

The next morning the ship got into the harbour
第二天早上,船驶入港口

they had arrived in a beautiful coastal town
他们来到了一个美丽的沿海小镇

on their arrival they were greeted by church bells
当他们到达时,他们受到了教堂钟声的欢迎

and from the high towers sounded a flourish of trumpets
从高高的塔楼上吹响了一阵阵号角

soldiers lined the roads through which they passed
士兵们在他们经过的道路上排成一排

Soldiers, with flying colors and glittering bayonets
士兵们,有着鲜艳的色彩和闪闪发光的刺刀

Every day that they were there there was a festival
他们在那里的每一天都有一个节日

balls and entertainments were organised for the event
为此次活动组织了舞会和娱乐活动

But the princess had not yet made her appearance
但公主还没有露面

she had been brought up and educated in a religious house
她在一个宗教家庭中长大和接受教育

she was learning every royal virtue of a princess
她正在学习公主的每一种皇室美德

At last, the princess made her royal appearance
最后,公主亮相了

The little mermaid was anxious to see her
小美人鱼急于见到她

she had to know whether she really was beautiful
她必须知道自己是否真的美丽
she was obliged to admit she really was beautiful
她不得不承认自己真的很漂亮
she had never seen a more perfect vision of beauty
她从未见过比这更完美的美
Her skin was delicately fair
她的皮肤非常白皙
and her laughing blue eyes shone with truth and purity
她笑的蓝眼睛闪耀着真理和纯洁的光芒
"It was you," said the prince
"是你，"王子说
"you saved my life when I lay as if dead on the beach"
"当我躺在沙滩上时，你救了我的命"
"and he held his blushing bride in his arms"
"他把脸红的新娘抱在怀里"

"Oh, I am too happy!" said he to the little mermaid
"噢，我太高兴了！"他对小美人鱼说
"my fondest hopes are now fulfilled"
"我最美好的希望现在实现了"
"You will rejoice at my happiness"
"你会为我的幸福而欢欣鼓舞"
"because your devotion to me is great and sincere"
"因为你对我的奉献是伟大而真诚的"
The little mermaid kissed the prince's hand
小美人鱼亲吻了王子的手
and she felt as if her heart were already broken
她觉得自己的心好像已经碎了
His wedding morning would bring death to her
他的婚礼早晨会给她带来死亡
she knew she was to become the foam of the sea
她知道自己会成为大海的泡沫

the sound of the church bells rang through the town
教堂的钟声响彻整个小镇

the heralds rode through the town proclaiming the betrothal
传令兵骑马穿过城镇宣布订婚

Perfumed oil was burned in silver lamps on every altar
每个祭坛上的银灯都燃烧着香油

The priests waved the censers over the couple
祭司们向这对夫妇挥舞着香炉

and the bride and the bridegroom joined their hands
新娘和新郎手拉手

and they received the blessing of the bishop
他们得到了主教的祝福

The little mermaid was dressed in silk and gold
小美人鱼穿着丝绸和黄金的衣服

she held up the bride's dress, in great pain
她痛苦地举起新娘的礼服

but her ears heard nothing of the festive music
但她的耳朵却听不到节日的音乐

and her eyes saw not the holy ceremony
她的眼睛没有看到神圣的仪式

She thought of the night of death coming to her
她想到了死亡之夜降临到她身上

and she mourned for all she had lost in the world
她为她在世界上失去的一切而哀悼

that evening the bride and bridegroom boarded the ship
那天晚上，新娘和新郎登上了船

the ship's cannons were roaring to celebrate the event
船上的大炮咆哮着庆祝这一事件

and all the flags of the kingdom were waving
王国的所有旗帜都在飘扬

in the centre of the ship a tent had been erected

在船的中央竖起了一个帐篷
in the tent were the sleeping couches for the newlyweds
帐篷里是新婚夫妇的睡沙发
the winds were favourable for navigating the calm sea
风有利于在平静的海面上航行
and the ship glided as smoothly as the birds of the sky
船像天空中的鸟儿一样平稳地滑行

When it grew dark, a number of colored lamps were lighted
天黑了，点亮了几盏彩色灯
the sailors and royal family danced merrily on the deck
水手和王室成员在甲板上欢快地跳舞
The little mermaid could not help thinking of her birthday
小美人鱼不禁想起了自己的生日
the day that she rose out of the sea for the first time
她第一次从海里升起的那一天
similar joyful festivities were celebrated on that day
这一天也举行了类似的欢乐庆祝活动
she thought about the wonder and hope she felt that day
她想起了那天她所感受到的惊奇和希望
with those pleasant memories, she too joined in the dance
带着这些愉快的回忆，她也加入了舞蹈
on her paining feet, she poised herself in the air
在她疼痛的脚上，她把自己放在空中
the way a swallow poises itself when in pursued of prey
燕子在追逐猎物时的姿势
the sailors and the servants cheered her wonderingly
水手和仆人都好奇地为她欢呼

She had never danced so gracefully before
她以前从未如此优雅地跳舞
Her tender feet felt as if cut with sharp knives
她柔嫩的脚感觉就像被锋利的刀子割伤
but she cared little for the pain of her feet
但她并不在乎脚的疼痛
there was a much sharper pain piercing her heart
有一种更剧烈的疼痛刺穿了她的心

She knew this was the last evening she would ever see him
她知道这是她见到他的最后一个晚上
the prince for whom she had forsaken her kindred and home
她为之抛弃了亲戚和家的王子
She had given up her beautiful voice for him
她为他放弃了她美丽的声音
and every day she had suffered unheard-of pain for him
她每天都为他遭受闻所未闻的痛苦
she suffered all this, while he knew nothing of her pain
她忍受了这一切,而他对她的痛苦一无所知
it was the last evening she would breath the same air as him
这是她和他呼吸同样空气的最后一个晚上
it was the last evening she would gaze on the same starry sky
这是她凝视同一片星空的最后一个晚上
it was the last evening she would gaze into the deep sea
这是她凝视深海的最后一个晚上
it was the last evening she would gaze into the eternal night

这是她凝视永恒之夜的最后一个夜晚
an eternal night without thoughts or dreams awaited her
一个没有思想和梦想的永恒之夜等待着她
She was born without a soul, and now she could never win one
她生来就没有灵魂，现在她永远无法赢得灵魂

All was joy and gaiety on the ship until long after midnight
船上的一切都是欢乐和欢乐，直到午夜过后很久
She smiled and danced with the others on the royal ship
她微笑着与皇家船上的其他人一起跳舞
but she danced while the thought of death was in her heart
但她跳舞时，她心中却有死亡的念头
she had to watch the prince dance with the princess
她不得不看着王子和公主跳舞
she had to watch when the prince kissed his beautiful bride
她不得不看着王子亲吻他美丽的新娘
she had to watch her play with the prince's raven hair
她不得不看着她玩弄王子的乌鸦头发
and she had to watch them enter the tent, arm in arm
她不得不眼睁睁地看着他们手挽手进入帐篷

after they had gone all became still on board the ship
他们走后，所有人都在船上静止了
only the pilot, who stood at the helm, was still awake
只有掌舵的飞行员还醒着
The little mermaid leaned on the edge of the vessel
小美人鱼靠在船的边缘
she looked towards the east for the first blush of

morning
她望向东方，寻找清晨的第一缕红晕

the first ray of the dawn, which was to be her death
黎明的第一缕曙光，也就是她的死亡

from far away she saw her sisters rising out of the sea
她从远处看到她的姐妹们从海里升起

They were as pale with fear as she was
他们和她一样因恐惧而脸色苍白

but their beautiful hair no longer waved in the wind
但他们美丽的头发不再随风飘扬

"We have given our hair to the witch," said they
"我们已经把头发交给了女巫，"他们说

"so that you do not have to die tonight"
"这样你就不必今晚死了"

"for our hair we have obtained this knife"
"为了我们的头发，我们得到了这把刀"

"Before the sun rises you must use this knife"
"在太阳升起之前，你必须使用这把刀"

"you must plunge the knife into the heart of the prince"
"你必须把刀王子的心脏"

"the warm blood of the prince must fall upon your feet"
"王子的热血必须落在你的脚上"

"and then your feet will grow together again"
"然后你们的脚会再次长在一起"

"where you have legs you will have a fish's tail again"
"你有腿的地方，你又会有鱼尾巴"

"and where you were human you will once more be a mermaid"
"在你曾经是人类的地方，你将再次成为美人鱼"

"then you can return to live with us, under the sea"
"那你就可以回去和我们一起生活了，在海底"

"and you will be given your three hundred years of a

mermaid"
"你将获得三百年的美人鱼"

"and only then will you be changed into the salty sea foam"
"只有这样，你才会变成咸咸的海沫"

"Haste, then; either he or you must die before sunrise"
"那么，快点；要么他，要么你必须在日出前死去"

"our old grandmother mourns for you day and night"
"我们的老祖母日夜为你哀悼"

"her white hair is falling out"
"她的白发脱落了"

"just as our hair fell under the witch's scissors"
"就像我们的头发落在女巫的剪刀下一样"

"Kill the prince, and come back," they begged her
"杀了王子，然后回来，"他们恳求她

"Do you not see the first red streaks in the sky?"
"你没有看到天空中的第一条红色条纹吗？"

"In a few minutes the sun will rise, and you will die"
"几分钟后太阳会升起，你会死的"

having done their best, her sisters sighed deeply
尽力而为后，她的姐妹们深深地叹了口气

mournfully her sisters sank back beneath the waves
可悲的是，她的姐妹们沉入了海浪之下

and the little mermaid was left with the knife in her hands
小美人鱼手里拿着刀

she drew back the crimson curtain of the tent
她拉开了帐篷的深红色窗帘

and in the tent she saw the beautiful bride
在帐篷里，她看见了美丽的新娘

her face was resting on the prince's breast
她的脸靠在王子的胸膛上

and then the little mermaid looked at the sky

然后小美人鱼看了看天空
on the horizon the rosy dawn grew brighter and brighter
在地平线上，玫瑰色的黎明越来越亮

She glanced at the sharp knife in her hands
她瞥了一眼手中锋利的刀

and again she fixed her eyes on the prince
她又一次把目光定在王子身上

She bent down and kissed his noble brow
她弯下腰，吻了吻他高贵的额头

he whispered the name of his bride in his dreams
他在梦中低声念叨着新娘的名字

he was dreaming of the princess he had married
他梦见了他娶的公主

the knife trembled in the hand of the little mermaid
刀在小美人鱼的手中颤抖着

but she flung the knife far into the waves
但她把刀扔进了海浪深处

where the knife fell the water turned red
刀落在哪里，水就变红了

the drops that spurted up looked like blood
喷出的水滴看起来像血

She cast one last look upon the prince she loved
她最后看了一眼她所爱的王子

the sun pierced the sky with its golden arrows
太阳用金色的箭刺穿了天空

and she threw herself from the ship into the sea
她从船上跳进了海里

the little mermaid felt her body dissolving into foam
小美人鱼感觉到她的身体溶解在泡沫中

and all that rose to the surface were bubbles of air
所有浮出水面的都是气泡

the sun's warm rays fell upon the cold foam

太阳温暖的光芒落在冰冷的泡沫上
but she did not feel as if she were dying
但她并不觉得自己快要死了
in a strange way she felt the warmth of the bright sun
她以一种奇怪的方式感受到了灿烂阳光的温暖
she saw hundreds of beautiful transparent creatures
她看到了数百个美丽的透明生物
the creatures were floating all around her
这些生物漂浮在她周围
through them she could see the white sails of the ships
透过它们,她可以看到船只的白色帆
and through them she saw the red clouds in the sky
透过它们,她看到了天空中的红云
Their speech was melodious and childlike
他们的讲话悠扬而充满童趣
but it could not be heard by mortal ears
但凡人的耳朵听不到
nor could their bodies be seen by mortal eyes
他们的尸体也无法被凡人的眼睛看到
The little mermaid perceived that she was like them
小美人鱼察觉到她和他们一样
and she felt that she was rising higher and higher
她觉得自己越来越高了
"Where am I?" asked she, and her voice sounded ethereal
"我在哪里?"她问道,她的声音听起来很空灵
there is no earthly music that could imitate her
世上没有音乐可以模仿她
"Among the daughters of the air," answered one of them
"在空中的女儿中,"其中一个回答
"A mermaid has not an immortal soul"
"美人鱼没有不朽的灵魂"
"nor can mermaids obtain immortal souls"

"美人鱼也无法获得不朽的灵魂"

"unless she wins the love of a human being"
"除非她赢得了人类的爱"

"on the will of another hangs her eternal destiny"
"在另一个人的意志上吊着她永恒的命运"

"like you, we do not have immortal souls either"
"和你一样,我们也没有不朽的灵魂"

"but we can obtain an immortal soul by our deeds"
"但我们可以通过我们的行为获得不朽的灵魂"

"We fly to warm countries and cool the sultry air"
"我们飞往温暖的国家,为闷热的空气降温"

"the heat that destroys mankind with pestilence"
"用瘟疫毁灭人类的热量"

"We carry the perfume of the flowers"
"我们带着鲜花的芬芳"

"and we spread health and restoration"
"我们传播健康和恢复"

"for three hundred years we travel the world like this"
"三百年来,我们像这样环游世界"

"in that time we strive to do all the good in our power"
"在那段时间里,我们努力尽我们所能做好事"

"when we succeed we receive an immortal soul"
"当我们成功时,我们会得到一个不朽的灵魂"

"and then we too take part in the happiness of mankind"
"然后我们也参与到人类的幸福中"

"You, poor little mermaid, have done your best"
"你,可怜的小美人鱼,已经尽力了"

"you have tried with your whole heart to do as we are doing"
"你已经全心全意地尝试像我们正在做的那样"

"You have suffered and endured an enormous pain"
"你受苦了,忍受了巨大的痛苦"

"by your good deeds you raised yourself to the spirit world"
"通过你的善行,你把自己提升到灵界"
"and now you will live alongside us for three hundred years"
"现在你将和我们一起生活三百年"
"by striving like us, you may obtain an immortal soul"
"像我们一样努力,你可能会获得不朽的灵魂"
The little mermaid lifted her glorified eyes toward the sun
小美人鱼抬起她那双光彩夺目的眼睛,望向太阳
for the first time, she felt her eyes filling with tears
她第一次感到自己的眼睛里充满了泪水

On the ship she had left there was life and noise
在她离开的船上,有生命和噪音
she saw the prince and his beautiful bride searched for her
她看到王子和他美丽的新娘在寻找她
Sorrowfully, they gazed at the pearly foam
他们悲伤地凝视着珍珠般的泡沫
it was as if they knew she had thrown herself into the waves
就好像他们知道她已经把自己扔进了海浪里
Unseen, she kissed the forehead of the bride
看不见,她亲吻了新娘的额头
and then she rose with the other children of the air
然后她和其他空中的孩子一起站起来
together they went to a rosy cloud that floated above
他们一起去了漂浮在上面的玫瑰色云

"After three hundred years," one of them started explaining
"三百年后,"其中一人开始解释道

"then we shall float into the kingdom of heaven," said she
"那我们就飘进天国了,"她说

"And we may even get there sooner," whispered a companion
"我们甚至可能更早到达那里,"一个同伴低声说

"Unseen we can enter the houses where there are children"
"看不见的我们可以进入有孩子的房子"

"in some of the houses we find good children"
"在一些房子里,我们找到了好孩子"

"these children are the joy of their parents"
"这些孩子是父母的快乐"

"and these children deserve the love of their parents"
"这些孩子应该得到父母的爱"

"such children shorten the time of our probation"
"这样的孩子缩短了我们的缓刑时间"

"The child does not know when we fly through the room"
"孩子不知道我们什么时候飞过房间"

"and they don't know that we smile with joy at their good conduct"
"他们不知道我们对他们的良好行为感到高兴"

"because then our judgement comes one day sooner"
"因为那样我们的审判就会提前一天到来"

"But we see naughty and wicked children too"
"但我们也看到顽皮和邪恶的孩子"

"when we see such children we shed tears of sorrow"
"当我们看到这样的孩子时,我们会流下悲伤的泪水"

"and for every tear we shed a day is added to our time"
"我们每流一滴眼泪,我们的时间就会增加一天"

The End / 结束

www.tranzlaty.com

www.ingramcontent.com/pod-product-compliance
Lightning Source LLC
Chambersburg PA
CBHW011953090526
44591CB00020B/2752